SITE SPECIFIC

ALSO BY ELAINE SEXTON

POETRY

Drive

Prospect/Refuge

Causeway

Sleuth

OPERA

The Post Office

After Stonewall

Elaine Sexton

Site Specific

new & selected poems

Grid Books, Boston

GRID BOOKS
Boston, Massachusetts
grid-books.org

Copyright © 2025 Elaine Sexton
All rights reserved.

COVER:
Amy Sillman
A Shape That Stands Up and Listens #26, 2012
Gouache, charcoal, and chalk on paper
22 in × 30 in (55.88 cm × 76.2 cm)
© Amy Sillman
Courtesy of the artist
Photography by John Berens

Design: John Kramer
Printed in the United States of America

ISBN: 978-1-946830-38-8
LCCN: 2024952841

for Nora

NEW POEMS

SLEUTH | 2003

CAUSEWAY | 2008

PROSPECT / REFUGE | 2015

DRIVE | 2022

NEW POEMS

The Work of Art

And here I am – an oil *on the edge of*
no place – night, or the edge of it,

a green that is always about to be
black – more trees, less light. And

the light of what sky there is –
glooms – and is almost always about

to go out. Here, a red horse marries
petrol in a sign where mythology

meets commerce. All this attention
to the sign lets the singleton by

the pumps and the road disappear.
Disappearance is both carriage and

parcel. Here is the *feel*, how wordlessness
finds its way – where my ear is pressed

to the present, my actual ear on
the literal pavement, on a country road,

here is where my seven-year-old face
prints experience on her skin, not

entirely smooth, but not rutted either.
Experience, so far and so deep, the past

is the dirt that isn't really dirt, and
gravel that isn't really rubberized

asphalt, but all that remains, pulverized,
a substance, a lesson in how roads

get made. Even in high season
some travelers will never find

this route, this short cut to the sea
(or me), or feel traffic

before seeing it, lying, flat, in a road,
the small in a small town, the edge

of this *curious half-dream, half-*
nightmare of somewhere to be

and nowhere to go.

figure & ground

> *"... there's an office in my brain full of people working at the same time I am talking to you ..."*

Sometimes I forget that plants are alive and hungry,
that the sky can be flat and expressionless, a soiled-
ceiling white. Let's mix metaphors, The most beautiful thing
about the past is a tongue on the glue of a stamp, time
and the envelope it comes in. Mail is fidelity. Paint is
translation.

Incandescence

And not just your wattage, your glow. Soft
white, warm, bright, daylight. Some lose
intensity, just dim ideas – warm, frosted,
long-standing. Some are chilly, young, clear,
and only offer an unwelcome florescence,
a blank stare striking a wall. Some are
insistent, unflattering, pressing, undressing
like a draft passing through glass
in a high-rise flat, wind whipping the dark,
so high up the sky seems to surround us.
Solitary, you stand or hang here
under a shade. Oh, bulb: don't ever
burn out. You are the last of your kind,
warm, inefficient, salvaged, dangerously
hot. I stroke the dust from your skull by day,
too hot to touch now it's too late to not
spend the night.

Small Points

Naturally, something that calls itself *small*
wants little to do with attention. Geography
called small is a quiet gush of light, tides
that pool in small sand-banked reservoirs,
and discreet stands of pines, the trees
not small, but their conversations are.
Hush of seals, their heads rise out of small
waves to gaze at each other and walkers
on the beach. Small snaps of seaweed,
and here on this slender (small) point
of stone and sand, a peninsula, almost silent
but for small bird calls. And you, present
in your skin, and your skin, dry, and
the wind, dry, small. And you, John Marin,
driving small points in long strokes, water
in your paint, the sea in your here, now.

on John Marin's "Small Point, Maine"

Time

is more beautiful than money.
Patience is more beautiful
than achievement. Green is
more beautiful than its absence
on a branch or the spine of a tree.
Red is more beautiful with
the sun bending and stretching
right on it, more beautiful peeling,
or about to peel,
where red has come to
rest on the west side of a clap-
board Cape in Maine, or
New Hampshire. And if enough
time has passed, this particular
red might be more beautiful
in proximity to a body of salt-
water marsh or a freshwater lake
that resides near a lightly trafficked
road alongside a woodland of scrub
pines or spruces or fir, and not so
remote that none could see it,
but right there so that anyone
could place their face their hands
right up close, so they could,
but wouldn't need to touch it,
to feel it, or see it like this
through paned glass
adjacent to it. Look. What could
be more beautiful than
this – time + patience,
with just enough light + color,
combined.

Last Night in the Country

The painter posted a picture of a dark sky
with a dark tree in it. The caption read:
"last night in the country." A statement
that is also a question. Early, in quarantine,
she made tiny abstract paintings, dashed
at her dining room table each night.
Did she mean it was her last night
in the country before returning to her
workspace in town? Or, did she mean this
was a picture she had taken *last night*,
and not the night before? And not
during the day. Did she mean she
was leaving *the country*, this country,
her body, her head, her family, and this,
a picture of her *last night* as
an American? She did not leave
the country, this country, with travel
severely restricted. She did not go
anywhere out of this world that day,
that night, but, maybe, in paint, in and
out of her head, in and out of her hand,
in and out of her house, in and out of
her body, her lover's, her pet's, her fields,
her knowing.

for Louise Fishman (1939–2021)

Screen Door

I can't stop hearing and touching its
splintering and yawning
its mothering its calling its bang
and air moving through its face
its trim never quite lining up
its wood its warp
its hook and eye
its new hampshire its beach
and flies caught in it
its passage its call back
its self-slamming shut
its banging and banging
and its spring
its longing to be pressed
its screws coming loose its green
paint peeling summer cottage hush
its winters in the basement
its basement its coming up for air
its robert frost its wallace stevens
its william carlos williams
its weeping its mind never
satisfied its roads diverging in a
wood its spine its sunshine
of late afternoon its doing
what it says it is going to do
the way it paints its own way
its draw its draft
its closing and not closing
its back door its back
to everything overgrown grass

on the other side of
its wrist its small knob
its metal its morning
its very early morning
it's always very early morning

Site Specific

Here, where I'm parked, the full
hot and cold sun is stuck, alone,
in its slot. There's no shade,
no sign of the time, memory's
gauge. Noon? Past? Where's my hat?
The moonroof is bent open.
I suck the air while I can, my lungs
let me. My phone remains un-
charged, while you, and you, and *you,*
whom I love are alive, so far
as I know. No news
can reach me. Bliss. This beach
remains unmapped. Here
I am empty, here, where I've never been,
where I've always lived, where waves crest
mission statements, which scatter
and repeat, and repeat, each time insisting
they love what they do, they love who
they are, they know what they know.

Inkhead – *a speaking part*

Carved in glass
with a pocket knife,
I am

I N K H E A D,
scratched in the window's pane,
one letter

at a time,
while the conductor
collects tickets

in other cars. My forehead,
my chin, the bridge
of my nose, my cheek bones

my lips, the crack
between my eye-
brows – a flash, a backdrop

from a train
that is field, a power-lined
sky, steam escaping a turbine

engine, clouds
anchoring air
only to be blown away

and replaced by rain
smearing my name. Honestly,
the process of discovery

is slow. I am presently
invisible, a rail-rider
unresolved, Oedipal

even,
pitching forward,
moving out

from in. I'm tempted
to leave it
at that.

But – drawing
while thinking –

I only just now
see the way ink
spends itself,

leaving, not
being
left.

Inkhead — *to caption a blur*

You are what a place means
to say about itself, if land
could speak as clear as, say,
color is translatable.
You are like all seeds — silent.
Something sorely troubled
my speech. The frame of its face
is still here, but the grit is gone,
what keeps us apart, a heaven
we could taste. Red
couldn't begin to explain
what blue is doing
in its veins. My face,
another story. We keep company
with roads that go nowhere,
or nowhere we ever
intended to go.

Fatigue

One lie masks another,
one fold carries a field
of folds, the truth's fine

fabric, porous
so you can see straight
through, all the way

to the Pentagon. One shield
holds another
in her chest, how to draw

a heart is the same
as the lungs. In,
out, in. Let the pulmonologist

rest, let her head stay
silent. No whirring, no
pumps, no prayers, just

rest.

Flight

Every day the same view is different
The blank sky is reflected in the devil's throat
Where the neck of one river
Reaches into another   the Harlem
Into the Hudson   All day
I sit in the sky   This high-rise is empty
Of thought   a container like any other
Container   piercing what was not there
Before   The sky   for example
At dusk bats thump along the tree line
Below   They know they're not birds

Mother in a Box

There's always room for the mother. She contains multitudes.
She is the shape we make when we mark pages
and paint, our complaints framed
by all that came before, before her mother, and her

mother before her. Here she is — the rim of a peony, petals
clinging to her stiff pink center, their lids holding still
before they open. Here she is — the mouth of June
porch steps, the past, where we sit tasting the sea we
don't see

but hear, touching salt air, the sun framed by
clothes lines, alive in mosquitoes, singing
and stinging in a box
which is slab, and tendency, which is memory, and
cemetery.

Memory Theatre

As the curtain goes up, we have emptied
a shelf of leather-bound books,
from a bookcase our not-long-
dead father built. We spread their bodies out
over the mustard-colored sea
of the living room rug. My brother is three.
I am five. The jacketless books form
an archipelago of worn-blue and fading-red
islands, with names we don't know
we can't read
yet. They are positioned for travel,
to step on, to cross over.

3 a.m.

All I want to do right now is sleep. And all sleep wants to do is lift its leg and pee on a tree. It cares nothing for me. Or the tree. I imagine I'm in charge. I try pulling it to the curb. Sleep is frisky and fretful, illusive and smooth. And withholding. Frankly, sleep needs me, all of me – just to be – but I'm the one who always gives in. When sleep presses, I cannot resist. It wants what it wants when it wants it. When I ask for sleep's favor in return, this one thing, this one time, when I truly need it – nothing. How many times will sleep break from its leash, run away, leaving me wired & tired, awake in its wake. It runs and runs, it runs a wild streak, so fast and so far, it's a dash, a fleck among flecks, in a dark forest or field, chasing rabbits, chasing sheep.

for Charles Simic

Tension

My brother texts to tell me to
look at the stars. Then asks:
do you have a compass? I packed a lot
for this trip to Maine, but not
that. He writes back: *find one*.

The first night of the new moon
is the best time to look. And I did.
Not knowing exactly
for what. What I did see, do see, clearly
is mystery – my brother looking up

at the stars, and me, looking up
at the same time, the same night,
the same stars. Recently he learned,
we learned, he has not long
to live. Every day, all day,

from this corner room
three or four (or more) flat-bed
trucks, full of timber,
rumble past. All week
I'd been calling this *lumber*.

A noun, and a verb. Today,
when I spell *timber* I hear a cartoon
character in a cartoon forest
shout "T-I-M-B-E-R," amber ax
in hand. *Timber* and *lumber*

are used interchangeably, but
timber is a felled tree
that still has its bark. Lumber
is milled wood, ready for building.
Timber gets more sympathy

from me. When I see these raw
bodies banded together, stacked
flat, ten feet high, I feel
their falling. I picture
them so close

in death. Lying flat in the flat-
bed of a truck, each tree's skin looks
the same as it did alive, a conifer
still standing up. For the tree
the back of a truck is not a bed.

A glen of them travel
on this road in an open coffin.
Their agency gone. *Agency*,
the one thing a character should have
on the page – alive – looking up.

Wait

I'm not waiting to be asked. I'm not
waiting for policy. I'm not waiting for
decency. I'm not waiting for positive
test results. I'm not waiting to lose
weight. I'm not waiting for
clean air. I'm not waiting for the noise
to die down, for hate to dissipate,
for class to not matter,
for greed to shut up. I can't wait
for the you in the poem
to show up, to be boring,
for the rain to come, to fall too fast
to pool in the road, to green
the trees, for time to be as common
and as generous as color
and the common cold.
I'm not waiting to be more awake
than this. Where do we go when we sleep?
when we can't? I can't wait to find out
where my dead are
living. I can't wait to find out
when I'll join them. And how. I'm not waiting for love
(thank god). I'm not waiting for grief (thank
no one). Here it is, bearing down, like breathing.
I'm not waiting for anything I don't have.
I have enough. When is everything not
enough, anyhow? I can't wait. I can't
wait to find out.

When It's Good to Stop Talking

i. *World Peace*

I solved all the problems, all
the road blocks

to world peace, yesterday, while
under the influence

at the dentist. And not
for the first time I can't remember

how, but the bliss of it remains
keen. I was changing

the world as the surly hygienist
informed me she would be

putting a bridge
in my mouth to keep the two

rows of teeth apart. I was thinking,
okay, *yes*, good to stop talking,

to open wide,
how even *this* bridge

brings things
together. You see how

it begins? I also solved the mystery
of the dysfunctional family,

and my reticence
to take in, fully, my brother's

relentless decline.
While under –

I dug and dug below the mystery
of disassociation, in time

with the strokes of a drill,
a soft rolling and rolling,

over and over each
tooth. And there, there it was,

all cleared up –
this fracture between us,

the past, the uncertain future
– gone. The bridge

remained. Tears fled
their traps, ducts

on each side of my face.
It happens a lot,

the hygienist said, *after* ...

When she asked *after* –

any questions?

Yes, I said, *yes*.

ii. Talking Politics

A beach is a river in my mouth.

Again, I go "under," a tiny cap
over my nose and the white
noise turns to an
ontological white, and the new
and kind hygienist
whose name, this time, is De Maris,
told me, *today*
was better than yesterday,
when I ask. Yesterday
the grave stone engraver
told her there would be a longer delay
to deliver the headstone
for her grandmother, Anna,
dead from covid, now, over a year.
De Maris said, in a chiseled English:

it is just not right.

While waiting for the drill I learned
her name is one she dislikes, one
her mother made up, with
two words. Her sister,
is Maris, and her mother,
just added the De,
and I think of my mother,
and *my* letdown, learning
my mother named me
after her nurse, after giving birth,
because it started with an "E."
Elaine, she prayed, in gratitude.

"of Mary?" I ask about the *De*
in *De Maris*. And she nods,
more alert
now to my mouth, of my making
a Mary of Maris, *the star*
of the sea. Laughing gas
works this way, I've come to
find out. I had just breakfasted with a friend, and,
as the air I breathed blanketed
my reserve, I swam into
my friend's stories of Mary and her search
for unlikely Madonnas in art.

Does Our Lady of Guadalupe
count? I ask, returning to the present,
to De Maris, to word
origins and the tricks they play
on the heart. *Adios*, for example,
doesn't only mean
good-bye. By now I'm going, going, *gone*
back to La Boca, a white mist,
an old barrio by a river in Buenos Aires,
I was young... younger. *Young*,
I go back to old friends *talking*
politics. I kept hearing
one after the other exclaim:
Gracias Adios! Ricardo first,
then Manolo, *gracias adios...*

I remember thinking:
thank you,
    goodbye?

It made no sense when nobody left.
The sweet stink of the used up
sewers and late night
streets of Argentina enveloped me.
It was so late and so dark,
the only thing to be thankful for
was the junta police eyed us,
asked us
for nothing. "*To god*," then,
I said, finally, to myself:

a dios, *de Maris*, *a dios*,
again, and again, in my head.
And by that time, the drill landed softly,
gently in my mouth. "Gracias
a dios," I tried to share my relief
with the dentist. *Thank god*, the fumed air
took me deeper and closer to
the more recent past, instead, grave
diggers, headstones, to my late brother's
carved box, whose ashes,
just last week, failed
to be tossed because no one thought to bring
a screw driver to open the lid
to his box
at the beach.

The dentist was asking if I was feeling
anything, touching my chin. I didn't
think he meant feelings
in the way I had been

exploring them now, glad
my mouth was frozen open,
so I couldn't and didn't say
I was afraid of not feeling
          a thing
all those months before
my brother's death, and the deaths
     of others.

About death I felt nothing,
          or not enough, then,
but I do now,
          and there won't be a
chiseled headstone
to remember my brother by.
Tiny bits of bone were gently, carefully,
made smooth to improve my bite,
but, just then,
                    I didn't feel a thing,
I thought but didn't say
to the closed captions
on screen over my head
          I didn't feel a thing
watching the ever-present war,
on the ubiquitous TV, or is that
the ever-present TV, and
the ubiquitous war? Words are wearisome
and blurry, even
out-of-focus, but the proximity to death
is present, and clear,
and not about to stop. I could see

from where I lay, the vague shape
of a very pregnant woman,
a Madonna, on a stretcher,
in a torn-up street, on screen,
a woman and her about-to-be-born
child, both I learned, later,
would die. If I went under, and stayed under,
and never came back,
I felt *Mary the star of the sea's* hand
pressing my shoulder,
gracias a dios
I had the words for this
after all—
and a drill in my mouth.

Poetry

When the air is this soft, when insects and
birds are the soundtrack, when your skin is
dried salt from the sea, and your clothes are
strung out on a line in a yard whose
path to the road is familiar and
empty and open to an ocean you hear but
can't see, whose wash is alive with
a friend who is dead, and has yet to confess
he will ever be otherwise, whose voice
keeps your grieving at bay, for the heart that keeps
breaking is yours, as the past co-exists with
the present, and this stand-alone moment is
cool, is safe, is no one you know is
suffering, or dying, or trying to, and this
intimate weather is real, is breathing, is
unasked-for, untethered, a place
where your heart and the heart you once
broke forgives you, and retreats to, after
exposing themselves like roadkill,
whose corpse threatens to upstage what
surrounds it, where you discover how
culpable and capable of cruelty
you can be, or have been, but also of practicing its
opposite, where time is now animate
and exceptional, but also reliably
unaccountably unkind.

Process

I count ferries like reading a clock,
clock/work, six days in a row, six ferries
in six hours, six observations
a day, every day, just to be clear:
rust, salt, snow, wild
turkeys in the yard, two
kayakers in the bay. In the winter
tree: one black crow.
The landlord left three
oranges to bloom in the bowl.
Eleven windows stay closed to the cold,
open to the water, sky, Little Diamond
and Great Diamond islands, at night
the lights of a small city, and those
of small jets after takeoff. An aging ferry
gave berth to our car. We are just now
being born to where the air scrapes
salt from the sea in a storm, off-season,
off-shore, off. And off. Just off. And
then on. The lights in the house.

Some notes on thoughts and where they take place.

a zuihitsu

Her doctors discovered a three-inch brain worm
was the cause of her previously un-diagnosable
distress. The pain was *not in her head.*[1]

"Ein Nagel im Kopf," a German expression:
"a nail in the head," commonly thought to suggest
a person is arrogant, eccentric.

The Nobel Prize winner told the *News Hour*
reporter: "lies in the news spread six times
faster than the truth."

Snail, snail, glisten me forward,
Bird, soft-sigh me home,
Worm, be with me.
This is my hard time.[2]

There is no "after" paradise.[3]

In the photo: My now-dead brother stands
next to a tree whose trunk is as thick as his.

The tree branches in two at eye level. Pressed
into the grooves of the bark, on the limb
furthest from his face – a string of white plastic
beads cinched together. And a white plastic cross.

It can never be satisfied, the mind, never.[4]

My dog's head is the size of my fist. He closes
his eyes and groans softly when I press my fingers
over the fur over the bones around his eyes, his snout.

---

1. *Science Friday*
2. Theodore Roethke
3. lost source
4. Wallace Stevens

Here, Neel

"Here, Neel brings her blunt, scrutinizing gaze to bear on her own elderly body, a gesture aimed squarely at an ageist, sexist society unused to seeing bodies like hers represented in fine art and popular culture."

—*from wall text describing "Self Portrait,"* Alice Neel: People Come First, *Metropolitan Museum of Art*

I think about what we are unused to seeing.
I think about bodies like hers.
I think about fine art.
I think about popular culture.

I think about a gesture aimed squarely at ageism.

" " " " " " " " sexism.

" " " " " " " " bodies like hers.

" " " " " " " " fine art.

" " " " " " " " popular culture.

I think about blunt.
I think about scrutiny.
I think about gesture.
I think about art.

Still Working

the coffee maker, the refrigerator,
the laptop and fountain
pen, the lamp from La Pampa,
and the wheelbarrow
with the broken leg. Still working –
the left wrist and the cracked rib.
What do ribs do – anyway? Still working:
the mnemonic device
which brings names and dates
into focus, cognition, and all it relies on:
you, and the memory of
school, and the dread of
father, and the idea of
absence, dead mother, and the way her
labor gathers like thread in my head. Still working, as in:
are you still? as in: all that question implies
when asked, as in: what makes
meaning, is it losing? Does the stomach still
break down acids and enzymes, do
the stars still reach their potential
to inspire, the larger the star the shorter its
life. Still working: the saw-dust and star-dust,
the poem as paper and ink, stain and light, broken
and mnemonic, still working
ribs and all.

Immunity

I dip my oar into the spring-
fed lake slicing
the ripple the breeze

makes, the breeze
inviting the skin
to relax and not worry

about sun, itself
reclining, recusing itself
from burning

anything up
so late in the day. Kay,
the elder,

is the anchor
behind me, her age
and complaints

steer the craft.
I can't look back.
Her poems, their pasts,

her pride, her
u n e x p r e s s e d
propels me further from shore

than her
confidence. I am less
able-bodied than I was.

In my palm the butt
of the old oar, exactly
correct. I press the base

of its arm, its fan, under water
then drag the fan
up. Inhale. Ex. You are here,

mother. I lift your eyes
with my own. I taste
the clean in the air

with your tongue.
The salt on my skin
is yours, breaking down.

I am always
breaking things down
dear breathing dear

lake dear
knowing dear
not.

Sound + Color

When weather snaps, cold + sun
is a welcome relief
from days of fog + rain,

though in fog we may see
what is not perfectly clear
when the sky is. Colors

stow in the fog. A Payne's grey
tug drives a barge
up river. A sedan, unlike

every other car, neither
black nor white, a blue,
manmade, ferries its driver

over the Henry Hudson Bridge
in the opposite
direction. It is easy to forget

the New Jersey Palisades
are all stone
covered by trees

you can't see. After foliage
retreats the volcanic rock,
basalt, stays. Some

of the words for stone
I find looking up.
The Lenape word is

weehawken:
cliff rocks that look like
rows of trees.

I find the folio in foliage,
trees are like books,
serial leafers.

If the tarps wrapping
and flapping
on the upper level

of the bridge are any indication,
the wind is coming
from the west. Three runners

bow into it heading south
on the lower level
leaving the *Half Moon*

overlook, the name
of Henry Hudson's boat.
They head into Manhattan,

cross the river also named
for the explorer, moving
in the opposite direction he did

setting out. They are stick figures
the color of shade. Eventually,
everything is shade,

which dulls color, but lifts it
the way fog does. Today,
this building casts

its shape the way,
if looking were fly fishing,
our eyes would plunge

like bait on a line,
over roof tops, span
the slope in the road, down

to the bridge whose base,
covered by trees, remains ever-
green. We'll see if it's true,

what I've said
about color. The sound
is the trees, whose pine leaves

sway and stay, like us,
accustomed to change.

All night the screen door slept

in the road, piecing together
scenes from its life swinging and
snapping shut, slaps and whines,
rusting and holding things back.

Transparency was always
its blessing and curse. No privacy,
security. Porous, letting in rain –
a toughness mosquitos and flies,
June bugs respond to.

Early on the screen earned a wooden cross
holding its frame when an elderly auntie
crashed through, chasing the dog
chasing the cat. Then, bars framed
its face. At last, something to push

and lean into. Open, then closed,
easily hurt, readily scarred,
the screen door knows who jammed it
with holes, splintered its frame to
complete its demise – the hook and eye

finally let go. Who bothers
locking a door one can see through?
The past and its lies.

Poetry is a tunnel

as aging is to breaking something. There's no fixing
age. True — the greater the age the freer we are to
drive our desires.
My last night in Rome, before heading home,
the last night in a month
of last nights in other cities, other towns, other
ruins, I kept counting and losing count
of what I did and did not do. The list kept losing
its height and shape. For one thing
I hate that I never found the words (in English)
for a text etched in a tunnel linking
the two ports of the same town, the old
and the new. I had days and days to do this.
The poet Montale paced those same streets,
in another century, measuring
and walking, and maybe getting lost,
gazing at the sea, the same sea,
il mare, the one word
no one needs to look up. Measuring and walking
and *greedy*, getting lost in Rome
I imagined *more* time,
even more time
off. With more, I would spend time
reading, not reaching.
I would be aimless. I would try not to
translate the *sky*, the way — in layers —
it falls off, the way it sounds like it would.
Is there even a word in English
for this? I crossed the city, the two sides
of the Tiber, over and back, travelers,

conjurers, pickpockets
orbit the Spanish Steps,
the empty and under-lit squares,
shops beginning to blush
after dark. After all the church visits, church art,
severed shoulders of saints, severed wrists of sinners,
I find art. Finding *new* art is like sinning
in a city so old, with the potential
for so much sin: lustrous light
and spilled paint, deliberate
and careless, beautiful and un-,
the blue-chip American gallery so close to
the aging and ageless Caravaggios
in their aging and ageless display.
The 15th century villa, made *shriekingly* new – showing
torn bits of paper, which are actually screens,
alive when the light hits their surface just right,
not far from the suffering and conversions
of saints, Peter and Paul, dimmed,
in their palace of worship,
at this hour empty of tourists.
I pay a euro to turn on the lights.

I was walking and chipping at an idea
of these monuments to commerce,
of aging, of beauty, of the Vatican, of Gagosian.
Between one famous piazza and my hotel,
in the clean, clear light of a one-room shop,
an old man handled a small head
broken open on a table, both head and table

the color of dust. Plasters & figures,
clocks filled his shelves. The bust
of a larger-than-life-size woman
with carved hair, cossetted and colorless,
her one elbow intact,
leaned over the artworker's head, hers
probably older than his, his
probably older than mine,
but just barely
older.

SLEUTH

Crime Scene

Nothing actual happened in the schoolhouse
girls' room on the island. It just looked like
something could. The scrubbed green & black
linoleum floors stretched under tubs and toilets
made of porcelain and closed up in oak stalls.
A mop & bucket in the corner might have been used
to disturb evidence. By mid-morning a weak light
pressed through the Coke-glass windows
set near the ceiling. "Made in America"
stained the bottom of spotless white basins
I examined in my hour of exile from lessons.
This is where I know the Sisters of Mercy
bathed naked on their summer retreats,
and later sent their failures – like me – to think
about sin. Without instruction. I sat on the rim
of a white tub and tried to make the connection
between evil and not remembering how to spell.
I gave up and resolved to be like Houdini,
to practice the trade of escape. This I would
learn to do with finesse. To be present, but gone.
The refinement came later. But now,
when the hall bell rang, my episode ended.
Recess brought dozens of girls, dressed like me,
swarming in. I flung my cell door open
and joined the flood of others in a rush
of pushing and flushing. I was spinning
in place, not knowing, exactly, what to do.
When no one was watching I forgot, and forgot,
and the forgetting, eventually, became me.

The Lid of Her Life

Her body is an empty address,
the journey's gone out of it.
Against tradition, I choose
not to look at the body.
I pace the park outside
and wait for someone
to close the lid.
That is not my mother in there,
I murmur to the stone monument,
the war dead of Portsmouth.
State Street, icy with snow,
melted, then frozen over.
I'll break my neck in these heels
I've put on to please her, the pearls,
her mink coat, right out of storage.

A Tongue on the Road

Here's the part of the Mass I hate, where
you have to say to strangers, in words

you'd never use in life, "Peace be
with you." When you do this you have to

embrace bodies in a way that's not natural,
not even at a party with cocktails. We are

bundled in coats. It is winter. The church
is stone. All through the gospel a young woman

two pews in front rubs her son's back,
then his head, his shoulders. She is tugging,

and tugs him closer and closer, tighter than
even he, clinging back, wants to be.

She searches his whole body to soothe him.
Or herself. I wish she would stop.

My mother is crying. I draw her temple
to my lips. She is mourning a loss, her

husband. She wants me to take Communion.
I won't. It's enough I'm here at all.

I look back to see who's in the balcony,
singing. I remember the toll booth attendant

last night on my long drive home
and imagine she says, "Go in peace,"

though mine is a journey she only takes fares for.
She is a god or a saint she doesn't know

she invokes. She trails, as all strangers do
in a dream. A tongue on a road,

empty, a speed dangerous
and high. She is a summons,

a siren. A chill in the night. Air.
a handout. An idea.

She is what it takes
to get there.

Hotel Recamier

Ten years later I could swear
the old orange spreads are now
curtains. We traded our double in back
for more light and this view. The narrow
single beds are brand-new and we
push them together, a familiar gesture,
the first night. The chambermaids
are used to this. They smooth out the sheets
every day, our way, spreading the blankets
sideways to cover the crack. I am at ease
with this, this time, but find it hard
to be here with someone else.
I did not plan on this very room,
the same cast-iron gate on the terrace,
the toilet, bidet, the same coarse towels,
faulty faucet. The water in Paris scalds me again,
this time for bringing you.

Lunch Hour

Harold and I were heartbroken when the old optical shop
closed and the rotating door with bronze pulls stopped
turning. We sat on a park bench in the shade of the Flatiron
by the empty corner store and box-shaped high-rise
built into it. When Restoration Hardware opened for business,
the shopping bags divided and new things made to look old
dropped in: rose-colored tumblers, stainless martini picks,
pince-nez with black ribbons, an hourglass no one will ever use.
Harold buys his Haitian cigars across the street, where painted
wood Indians, Native Americans, stand on display.
Today the pretty blonde who serves him, a flirtation he savors,
shows us a picture of her live-in girlfriend, a dark beauty
she keeps in her hip pocket, under plastic, in a century-old
wallet, hand-stitched, a gift her grandfather gave her.

The World Book

Here's the idea, silkworms spinning in the shade
of paper parasols, on dusty streets in home movies,
where my sisters actually have to dip under
blossoms to see. And steel shadows, their dark
rungs, glide by me, me swaddled in pink cloth
rising *blip blip blip* up the cinematic center of a
skyscraper in the City of Lights, and elsewhere
waves crash under our windows, and the tower is
bent, and there's row after row of scent. We're in
so many places, an encyclopedia might be tempted
to look *us* up. Kyoto, Fort Knox, Pittsburgh, Pisa,
Rye Beach, Melrose, Amsterdam, Paris, Verdun,
Ipswich, Fort Devens and more. Could I get more
specific? There, where my father died, where they
met, where my brother, John, was born, where
I was born, where *they* lived, where *we* lived,
where we *almost* lived, where he, my father, was
born, where my mother was small, where for me,
and for good, the whole world opened up. There,
where my mother went door-to-door, but not too
often. When she had to, she stopped. After all her
friends & neighbors bought. Where she tried to sell
The World Book to those she'd never met, who'd
never seen what she had seen, where Joan of Arc
was burnt at the stake, where pilgrims left their
crutches, where soldiers raped the virgins of war,
found giant conch shells to take home, where the
kings of France were crowned, that cathedral, my
baptismal site, where blessed water was dripped
over my head. And years, not too many years, later

the hands that held me over that Gothic font and lifted me past its iron grates knocked on the blank doors of strangers in Rye Beach. And only now, today, when we look up "gingko" to see how that old herb might restore her memory in this blue bound *World Book*, under the letter "G," she says to me so I see her feet at the threshold where she stands and her eyes stay, *Elaine*, she says, looking back, maybe, for the first time, as if thirty years were enough to lift any ordinary shade, *those doors were so big.*

The Flag of My Disposition

The free end of the flag snags in a beak
at the top of the pole. It tears and tears,
caught in a gust. The stripes strain, the threads
shred with each angry twist. This sail snaps
to nowhere. A mean wind takes me there.
Where everything stalls. Even a blow
gets marooned, and stars won't move.
They stare and stare from where they're fixed.
Right there, where the same groove gets deeper
and deeper. Hear that clink of the rope?
It's not a way out. But the same thin way in.

Sleuth

I become type on the page, Nancy Drew,
girl detective, solving mysteries

in a series of plots from the tower of books
by my bed. Downstairs the bookcase

my father built, too packed to hold mine,
holds his: *Mein Kampf* in German,

Greek classics, Russian grammar,
an atlas bound in leather,

the entire *World Book*. My father is dead.
I know him by what he collected

and read. He lives in Kodachrome film,
home movies, in his cufflinks, fountain pens,

in the stuffed sea turtle that swims in dust
in the basement. I learn nightly the secrets

of reading. The code. *The Clue in the Crumbling Wall*,
The Witch Tree Symbol. I play the part of Nancy

in the woods by our house, reenact *The Quest
of the Missing Map*, find sense in a tree's bark,

in letters my father wrote my mother,
in what she wrote back, wartime lovers.

Had my father lived, he might have sought my advice
the way Nancy's seeks hers, confiding his conflicts

in private, in his den. I prop my chin on the page,
follow the mystery of a father in fiction,

guiding his daughter, of my father guiding my mother,
in love. Nancy is forever missing a mother;

I cling to mine. I learn how my mother cuts patterns
for dresses in the kitchen, how she lands planes

from a tower as a WAC. My father is forever
missing. I puzzle over how this comes together

in print. I uncover new words, a girl named George,
villains in bungalows. Nancy rushes to the crime

scene in her yellow roadster in my head.
I dismantle my father's wireless recorder

on the porch, his voice too rusty to catch when
liquid mercury breaks from a glass tube inside,

and folds, cold, in my palm. I let it bead on Formica.
Nancy needs no one. I like this idea. Her father

needs *her*! She is fearless and calm. She makes
men tremble. I torment my brother, who grabs

at this magic I play with. We're stunned to see
mercury sucked from his hand, swallowed

whole in the pores of his ring, my father's.
The Mystery of Alchemy in reverse, the gold band

turns silver and mute. Nancy finds a home
for an orphan, an heiress, her fortune.

I discover the cost of curiosity;
I have the tools for detection.

Nancy has what she needs, she's forever eighteen.
The Mystery of the Tolling Bell unfolds.

I don't know till the last page, the last line –
whom to trust. Each day I betray the secrets

of the white clapboard house where we lived,
the mystery of the missing keys to our untuned piano,

the reason a life-size statue of the Virgin Mary
sways in the trunk of the car, today,

as we drive to the dump. Memory is murky.
I follow the clues, the words, the quest for the dead,

for the father, the daughter always led by the author,
the flashlight as it moves in her head.

Totem

She once stood up between pines, a symbol
of faith I didn't buy—the Virgin Mary,

her stone toes buried in tiger lilies.
She rests now in the trunk of my car

on the way to the dump. Her placid gaze,
her image always an embarrassment,

a joke, a landmark for finding our house.
Her body a monument caught in headlights at night

as my dates turned their cars in our drive.
One summer Aunt Dorothy from Pittsburgh

painted Mary's flesh pink, her robes blue,
and my job was to wash her back

to white. The virgin came with the house
bought from another aunt: Ruth, the ex-nun.

The day we climbed out of the Rambler
into our new yard, my brothers found

the chicken coop, my sisters the basement.
I hung on the statue, picked pine cones

at her feet. We ran from the house
down the road to the beach.

This was our new life without a father.
We learned how to keep my mother

in our hip pockets, wrap her tight
around our little fingers. We stopped kneeling

by our beds to pray before sleep and indulged
in our fears, our imaginations. We heard

the hazards of riptides, how an orphan
from Boston drowned under our aunt's care,

how the Mother of God was placed in the yard
to make amends. *How could it?* I'd ask her,

mouthing the words to deaf ears, her carved veil
unmoving. Every day I crossed her path to post

the mail. Sand and salt from the beach
stuck to my legs. The summer I was ten

she was exactly my size. Some days I'd balance
my feet on her base, wrap my body around hers,

taste plaster splintered down her spine.
I'd whisper: *Where's my father?* Or

Find my mother a new husband.
I knew it was voodoo, even then.

Enclosures

I dig for replacements in her button box.
Sometimes a bit of fabric clings

to the metal backing of a clasp,
a perfect match hangs by a thread.

I hold the past lives of apparel, a snap,
an embroidered enclosure

in my head. I retrieve every part
of a torn blouse, a worn vest

she stripped for parts, pearls
snipped from a bodice, bone knobs

cut from their beds. An old zipper
lines the back of a new dress.

Lace and elastic seek re-employment.
I run my palm over jagged teeth,

unmatched seams of a striped shirt.
I dust my mother's shiny black Singer,

her foot on the pedal, the hum she'd
retreat to, the needle and the bobbin.

Code

He was dining at sea with friends
when it happened. His invention.
The telegraph. Samuel Morse. The Morse Code. He was manic,
depressive, an artist. He was frantic, rigid, impolitic.
He ran for mayor and lost. He hated Jews and Irish.
He found abolitionists demented.
He made gardens. And would not quit
until Congress approved. His method. It changed
everything. Made him famous. He painted
and hated portraits. He lectured
and married his cousin. He sued. And won,
and was rich. The code is retired, now. A satellite
relays distress signals that once defined
distress. The sound
and light. The language.

Little Boar's Head

cuts into the coast, a snout of stone
licks the sea back each time it is hit.
This is how a shape gets its name.
The point in the road turns
angry, just a little mad,
so your hairs bristle a bit
at the bite the Atlantic is taking.
Time takes shape for granted.
I wait for the swoop the car
makes with us in descent,
what we call a hairpin
in romance or detective fiction.

Super 8

We are waving, swimming,
waving, the salty mounds break
over our heads. We are waving,

kicking, swimming, the sea grass
sticks to our legs. We are leaving,
waving, drying our faces on towels

pulled from the line. Wet hair sticks
to our skin like sea grass, the salt
dries like snow on a shell.

The Trade of Escape

The film star drops out of the sky
when his prop plane loses an engine,
Tupac is shot, and his body-
guard, too. Both items are news
you hear as you wait on hold
on the phone in the office. The radio
broadcasts a mixture of sun & clouds
you can't see without windows.
The West Side Drive is backed up
for miles, a twenty-minute delay
expected, outbound
at the Williamsburg Bridge
and the Mid-Town Tunnel. Today
you rummage in your desk for an aspirin,
while the call you made makes you wait.
You draw small crafts in the margin
of a yellow pad, and forget who it is
you have called. Boats with outboard
engines, a float plane with its single propeller,
coast on a Pilot pen's ink. Little black swells
form to a tune by Vivaldi that replaces
the news. A willow tree drops its weeping
leaves down on one side of the page, and by now
you've left the building, the city.
The letters and phone have become
props in a stage for departure. How many
wings will it take to lift you, intact, over
the side of your cube by the mail room?
Every day deliveries come and go. Express,
Overnight, Second Day, Same Day. One day
a courier asks you which way is out,
and you follow the directions you gave him.

The Pitch Forward

This is a type of extreme sport. A three-inch
"S" hook fits on the far limb of an elm tree,
my thighs pressed against the fire escape
so my hands stay free to hang a birdhouse,
your gift from the farm. I slip on the grate,
alone, catching myself and the bag of seed
before one of us drops three flights to the yard
below. I am dressed especially for climbing
out the window. I scrape my knuckles
the first time out. This is how I pitch
forward this morning. I leave
the rapids of my last great romance behind.
The past is the raft I let go. Some days
falling for you is a walk in the woods,
watching Great Blue Herons mate in the pines,
their stick legs drifting. Two osprey sail over us,
suspended in air. An old trick of theirs.
All the birds travel in pairs. Nothing too risky
in that, I say to myself, putting the sooty screen
back in the frame, the window refusing to shut.

Building a Nest

She fit the printed tissue pattern
flat over my chest, her fingers
lining the place where the seams go,
a circle over my shoulders, under my arms,
down my spine. The shapes she cut later
in fabric – seersucker for summer, boiled
wool in winter. This morning you press your hands
on the pale cotton sheets over my ankles
where the inseams go between my legs,
your lips pursed like my mother's, full of pins.

Public Transportation

She is perfectly ordinary, a cashmere scarf
snugly wrapped around her neck. She is
a middle age that is crisp, appealing in New York.
She is a brain surgeon or a designer of blowdryers.
I know this because I am in her skin this morning
riding the bus, happy to be not young, happy to be
thrilled that it is cold and I have a warm hat on.
Everyone is someone other than you think
under her skin. The driver does not have
a peanut butter and jelly sandwich in his metal
lunchbox. He has caviar left over from New Year's
and a love note from his mistress, whom he just left
on the corner of Sixth Avenue and 14th Street.
When she steps off his bus to take over the wheel
of the crosstown No. 8, she knows she is anything
but ordinary. She climbs under the safety bar
and straps the belt on over her seat. She lets
the old lady who is rich but looks poor take her time
getting on. She lets the mugger who looks like
a parish priest help her. She waits as we sit, quiet
in our private, gorgeous lives.

Rethinking Regret

Let's thank our mistakes, let's bless them
for their humanity, their terribly weak chins.
We should offer them our gratitude and admiration
for giving us our clefts and scarring us with
embarrassment, the hot flash of confession.
Thank you, transgressions! for making us so right
in our imperfections. Less flawed, we might have
turned away, feeling too fit, our desires looking
for better directions. Without them, we might have
passed the place where one of us stood, watching
someone else walk away, and followed them,
while our perfect mistake walked straight towards us,
walked right into our cluttered, ordered lives
that could have been closed but were not,
that could have been asleep, but instead
stayed up, all night, forgetting the pill,
the good book, the necessary eight hours,
and lay there – in the middle of the bed –
keeping the heart awake – open and stunned,
stunning. How unhappy perfection must be
over there on the shelf without a crack, without
this critical break – this falling – this sudden, thrilling draft.

CAUSEWAY

Turnstile

I carry the prints of a hundred thousand
strangers in my hands, their palms
on the turnstile this morning like mine
touching the kiosk buttons, fingering
coins to pay for the *Times*. At Union Square
Station, the stale breath of others
inhabits the boxcar air. The scent of lilacs
shuttles with us from the garden to work
with our spring colds, our smokers' coughs,
the *Daily News* the others left behind
on their seats, vacant, invisible debris,
tubercular, airborne like grief, theirs
not like mine, not like anyone else's.

Lower Manhattan Pantoum

Always a bad sign
people on the sidewalk looking up.
A crowd forms, cars slow
then stop,

People on the sidewalk looking up.
I step into the pool of them
then stop.
I gape like the others.

I step into the pool of them,
become the pool
and gape like the others.
Mothers, peddlers, suits

become the pool
of a wreck.
Mothers, peddlers, suits,
my super, my neighbors,

a wreck
unfolding, undone.
My super, my neighbors,
no one is not stunned.

Unfolding, undone,
we look at our watches,
stunned.
Someone says *let's pray.*

We examine our watches.
A crowd forms. Cars stop.
Someone says *let's pray* —
always a bad sign.

Masonry

Brick of my mother's
Pittsburgh, her
weather steel-mill gray
every day, brick
of my father's Boston
law school at night,

the Federal brick
of Portsmouth, New Hampshire,
where I pined for a boy
at a brick ferry landing
and flirted
with sailors and prayer

but gave up
every brick
of every seaside city
I lived in,
so nearly the same:
Newport, New-

buryport. The whole
Eastern Seaboard's
worn bricks
crumbled alike
in the sun. Urban brick,
in particular,

the brick shelters
of love. New York
City brick, best of all,
the West Village brick,
more precisely,
where I bricked up

one life and tore it down,
one love, then
another, no more

stable. Or just as stable.
One brick at a time.
Brick of desire,

brick of loyalty, brick
of empathy, brick of guilt,
of solitude,
brick by irregular
brick.

Night. Fire.

When we looked up after hours of staring
at a crimp in a log, the shooting blue
flames, puffs of smoke,
the tide that was right here had gone
way out, so the waves were now strokes of gray
in the distance, and the dark night closed in
on us, everywhere at once.

Everywhere at once the sky was touchable,
for of course it was right here, over us,
as well as way out over the smaller and smaller waves,
coming forward but still going out.

Coming forward but still going out, leaving
us to watch this crashing in and in
yet each time receding, the way our conversation
happened along those same lines.

Along those lines we managed a few
untouchable subjects, the way we imagine
we can touch a star or the moon on a night like this
but know we really can't. We imagine we see
everything more clearly, but that doesn't work
with the past. Which is what we were dealing with,
in the way families try to deal with this sort of thing.

Families deal with this sort of thing
poorly, so far as I can tell, and so when the bon-
fire loosened its hold and we stretched our mysteries out
over the sand, the way we'd never do over a meal
in one or the other's house, we heard

the lips of one wave touch another as if each spoke for us.
And words came slowly, or didn't come at all.
Slow, or sometimes not at all, seemed better
than never. And never seemed to be coming
forward like the sky, which is always so close
and receding at the same time.

Estuary English

A sea-mark exposed my limits.
This is where loss first
opened its mouth, where
my alongshore navigation
began. I was practically born
in a tide pool, the wrack
of my family, a view
best seen in words, buried
like a razor-necked clam, my shell,
part of some bigger mystery,
solid enough to call home but not
too hard to crack. In the beak
of a gull, the earth finally showed
its shape. One minute
I swam in the sand, the next, wings
beat over my head; the sweep
of the coast showed below, lineated
as I never imagined. I hung
in the firm grip of two claws, fear
and desire. I did nothing but let them
hold me. I struggled little
once I caught sight of waves cresting
and crashing. It made no sense,
given the gravity of granite,
not to look, and keep looking.

Onion Field

Our friends wanted us to taste everything:
their dust and sweet air, their mangy
Mexican dogs, banana leaves floating,
botanical, architectural. Here, they trade
mostly roses, fields and fields of their bodies
for sale in red bundles like firewood
on the road. Here, where the barb
in the barbed wire fence
caught me, onions roasted on a grill
with clusters of chilies I never dared touch
with my tongue. Only a small thread of me
kept snagging and unraveling as crops turned,
and miles and miles of fence
framed beauty like something lit by a match.
Did I know, even then,
our friend and driver, our host,
would die, months later? And you,
whom I love, I would leave.
And the house where we stayed, year after year,
down a lane cut through onion fields,
would be sold. That I'd actually risk
not coming back to this place. Again. And again.

A Bird in the House

1.

The knocking and knocking
in her washing machine
brought things sharply into focus
when I raised the lid and saw her daily laundry:
a single bra, its metal clasp
hitting the walls of her white Kenmore
over and over. I said, *mother, there's nearly*
nothing in here. She busied herself at the sink
full of dishes unwashed for a week.

Shopping for bras that afternoon,
I joined her in the dressing room.
She couldn't remember her size.
Not being a mother, I saw how I'd never know
the coming-of-age of a daughter, but,
instead, I'd be a daughter helping my mother
measure this gentle harness,
the first of many stays
we'd share and let go as she needed me.

2.

Late one night my mother called my brother:
a bird in her house and she couldn't get it out,
even with her broom. He raced the dark mile
over the causeway and found no bird,
though together they thumped through every room.

She swore *there is a bird, there is a bird in the house*,
and the bird in her house was something
we whispered between us all week.

Mother, there is no bird, we said.

There is a bird, she said, *there is a bird*,
the first of many repetitions.

Maybe you know how this goes.

We turned back the clocks,
and the days turned mysteriously cold
along with the light. Her house, full of shadows,
showed how fear might draw a bird in the house.

I decided to visit more often.

A week later, alone with my mother,
I snapped on her light in the hall. An enormous
black bird knocked its frantic wings on the walls,
clawing the air over our heads.

I opened the heavy front door. It flew out.

Office Sonnet

To Ted on the other side of my cube:
I'm sorry your mother does not
remember you called her ten minutes ago,
and I'm sorry you have to move her
from her home, the one you grew up in.

And even though we have never spoken
about anything but the weather and
spikes in the news, I'm sorry you have no
privacy, and I'm sorry you have to listen
to me schmooze with my lover, long distance,

and honk business on the phone
every day. I hope your retirement plans
work out, though no one is supposed
to know. Your secrets are safe with me.

Village Butcher

I consider the sun scorching the sidewalk
where I live, where I exact
a living wage of pleasure
each morning. Whether I want to or not,
I get up. I judge my life the way
the butcher, two blocks away,
gauges the weight of prime rib
in his shop, precisely, without measure,
as he does this morning
slicing fat, dressing the slab
as if prime rib were an ode he is writing
to food. He examines his life
between slices. Conscious.
Alone. He's outlived his father,
his mother. He inherits the store.
He answers the phone
and wipes blood from his glove –
while I wait – glad to be loved
by someone he clearly loves back.
He stands, knife in hand,
and considers her voice, the chords
as they climb through her mouth,
then his, then mine.

Causeway

Outside your idea of me
I stray. I keep to myself
as much as anyone can
keep to herself
beside you. You, sniffing,
like a rat catcher,
like a terrier that is friendly
until it catches some
thing run amuck.

Walking the causeway,
I'm invisible, stirred
under the radar
of your thinking,
where I snag and catch myself
wanting to be
somewhere else,
not here, where
the marsh and bay
divide at our sides.

Here I hide like a dog,
like the rat catcher I am.

Below, scratching the sand,
even the tiniest crustacean
finds a place other than her skin
to retreat to. The hermit crab,
squeezed in a shell,

contorts her own body
to carry the weight
of a hard-won
scholarship on her back.

First Person

In the rearview mirror an egret
lifts off from swamp grass;

in the driveway you wave me away.
I leave the original way, in person.

But you, remembered, are sharper,
more beautiful in the poem, carried

this way, the way a playwright
might feature your gestures

in the act of the heart breaking
over and over so the sound of the heart

breaking is sharper and more
beautiful than the original heartbreak,

so nearly unbearable you'd never
wish to feel it, directly, again.

A Psalm Sung by a Fish

Heady is the current that carries us
without exertion,
undetected,

the absence of refuse. Sublime,
the trapless bay,
the boatless harbor,

the green-gray waves
cresting overhead.
Auspicious, the airtight oil tanker,

the honorable sea captain,
the righteous longshoreman
standing watch

over the docks. Humble
are those who navigate
this spring migration. The fish

hawk scans the shore, circles back.
Surely she sees us. Lucky
for the flash that teased her

to pass—if I had a knee
I'd bend it in thanks. Fish
are not known to believe,

but I might be
persuaded,
living this long,

traveling this far
on the earth
in the sea.

Recovered Blue

Speck of a shell
no bigger than

an acorn nib
attached to my skin

after a swim, a sliver
from a mollusk's

lodge, bluer
than any painted blue,

deepest when wet,
hollowed by salt.

Splinter, sorrow,
a structure from which

even the sea
has been taken.

Monoprint of a Shoe

Tongue, heel, sole,
laces and eyelets, oh shoe
on a flatbed, dissected,
these parts are not
the sum of your whole

life, the grass and the gravel,
the snow, the mud we've met.
The soot that collects
in your cracks is
age, polished, the scent

made soft, your body
misused, laid
under a bed, dumped
in a closet. Oh valued
companion, now finished,

accessory to crimes,
the commitment of living:
to the graveside,
to the wedding, to work,
to the station.

You are the conditions
taking me. You fit my step.

Deciding to Walk

Because I couldn't find the subway
right away, because the night air
was the softest it's been
in a year,

suddenly lonely, without a plan
and no friend to call, and
wanting to feel this
clearly,

last night I decided to walk
home forty blocks
past tourists making
memorial signage,

past the post-disaster
cleanup into
after-work chatter wafting

from darkened bars
into the stink of junkie
pharmaceutical waste

on cracked pavement.
I could have chosen the *new* New York,
listing along the Hudson,
her kayak armada,

her encouraging bike paths,
azaleas, evergreened landfill.
I could have let my spirits be lifted,
but I wanted to taste the city

where little remains
undocumented,
the grit left out of these plans
for the new world order.

Collage

After the opening, after
the toasts and first courses,
after the strands of our past
lives meet & unravel,
we discover we *are*
the middle-aged strangers
from New Jersey
who join us, torn
from another century,
names changed, accents lost,
new ones acquired in the boroughs,
in Manhattan, artists
and working class, heroes,
clerks, and collector
tycoons. These small-buttoned
landscapes — a grid, a map
pecked out in ticket stubs
coat checks, pins and needles
pointing, warning labels,
pulled from their pillows — become a collage
of benign signs. Even in these
toxic times, we live, we thrive.

Taken

This is the boat that took me
out of my marriage,
the painter said, then clicked

to the next slide. Here is the chair,
the spare table I pulled my grief
up to. Here is where the gash

of oil paint put me: behind
a door closed, thick green
strokes refusing to leave.

Heaven

When my sister lifted the World War II
Army-green flight suit
from a bag, our dead mother,

as WAC, stepped into her empty
pant legs, returned to us
quiet as dust. We carried her up

from the basement. Mice, nesting
in waves of wrinkled wool, left
teeth marks in fabric. Her wartime

wedding band's vines
curled in my palm with an old rosary
blessed by Pope Pius XII

for my mother, a pregnant
believer, in Rome.
Still, I refuse to pray

on dead wood. Some days,
I confess, I caress a circle
of painted orange beads

with a coconut cross I bought
in a zócalo market. Sometimes
I find them to finger

in secret, walking home
from work in Manhattan. Once
I found them in a winter coat pocket

on a plane as the workers de-
iced the wings. You might call this
a prayer, a return to that moment,

that year I believed God
lived in Mexico's mountains.
Trees rushed the sky

as the sky itself
gathered thousands of migrating
monarchs. I saw them lift off,

saw the shape of my body, leaving
my body, on a ridge. My body
as air. Not one I'd known,

or had ever known. Not one
I'd seen, or had ever seen
before this.

The Horse in Her

The horse in her led us into the wood,
crossing paddock and fence, over creek
and fallen oak, where the stark sun leaked
between branches more and more barren
with every gust of wind. The weeping leaves,
prescient and thick as they filled the hollows,
fell faster and faster as they stuffed
every place we looked down to for balance.
Steady at 80, she led us, shifting
her legs over a thick trunk
blocking the path, intent on finding
the mushroom grove a mile deeper in.
Their white heads, as she predicted,
peered from a lunar bed freckling the sweep
of pine needles, orange, between roots
of rotted trees. The soft space invited her
to fold and roll her body down, knowing
if one horse rolls the others follow.

for Maxine Kumin

Pollyanna Redux

My spin turns loss
into asset

and twists in the maker
who casts me

alone with the evil aunt
in the attic room,

who makes me
glad to get crutches

for Christmas, glad
not to need them.

I had to lose
my mother, my father,

otherwise there'd be no
silver lining, no cliché

to make bearable
the everyday obscene.

I'd like a word with the author.
I'd like to tell her: grow up!

I'd like to tell her:
today

I plan to be unforgiving.
I plan to be inconsolable,

just once. I plan to stop
reinventing the father,

the substitute mother.
I recruit my old friends

in fiction. Orphans, originals:
Heidi rethinks her trek

up the Alps. Snow White
reclines in a slump.

I call Cinderella,
who places Prince Charming

on a shelf. We unearth
the sour, the bitter, the selfish,

our collective
unuttered umbrage.

Together, we stew the past
and make a boil out of it.

Magnolias

You reach, thick and flush, over sidewalks
to inhabit the air, Brooklyn, spring
before summer suckles the breeze
out of it. Your arms, a former lover's,
classic and damaged, a South America
that could have been Paris, but isn't:
civilized, democratic, but never new
like the New World suggests. Each day
a steamship of possibility. All I see
is the blue in your magenta, your pitted
sorrow, your South, waiting to wake,
a pulse, dim, but still there, blue
lines under your thick shell.

“Lake Camp”

I regret
I did not buy

your small
looked-over landscape.

Thick paint
now occupies

that part of the brain
I retreat to –

the small boat,
a black stroke after sunset;

your pines, foothills,
the lake itself –

brown shades
at this hour.

Only the frame
is darker.

I inhabit the sliver
of light – left on –

in the cabin:
bone white.

PROSPECT / REFUGE

Only Sky

You walk not rush into these
pictures, the way you step into air
leaving the house,
leaving the door still open.

What you see is all sky
with a skid of land, a tree-
line, or the dark eddy
of sea lapping over

the foreground, or just
pulling back. If you asked,
I'd say all that oxygen
answers every quarrel

we have with ourselves, each
dissolves in the face
of space, the way a stain
in the sky

makes us want to
stop the car, stop *thinking*,
call a friend to
come out of her house,

her kitchen, leave the burners on,
but come *now*
because beauty is likely to burn up
the minute you turn your back.

You know *life is long*
a friend once offered.
A perfect lie. And who
doesn't think of a flame

when something
embezzles
your breath,
beating

like the memory of taste
or echo of a color
on air.
Only this time

the sky is my witness
as it is most of the time
which is to say
all the time I am alone.

Cantilever Love

This plank, observation
deck of the great Minneapolis
high-rise theatre
reaches out
to the Mississippi
and Saint Paul,

Pillsbury's smokestacks,
so close they are
almost touchable,
the mother/structure,
left behind, sturdy,

weight-bearing,
safe. I stand, suspended,
midair, on metal/cement,
cantilevered. So much depends
on what we can't touch.

I reach my face
over the edge, past
glass barriers. Spray
from the great river reaches back.
We almost touch. Tender.

Architectural.
I've come here in splits,
jerry-rigged,
insupportable.
It's touching the way

the body keeps
trying, the body
built to house the brain,
the brain built to house the senses,
the senses themselves

containment facilities,
at once restless and
content to flare up,
die out. Some,
in cantilever moods,

step out. The sun
fixes itself on the skin
which, in turn, contracts
the way the optic
nerve does. In the dark

white jasmine
opens, and exhales.
Hairs in the nose,
tiny cantilevered planks,
reach out to carry

the scent
back to the brain.
My tongue, cantilevered
from my mouth,
touches the fine down

on the nape of your neck
and lifts
not exactly a flavor
but an idea,
suspended, blindfolded, balanced.

Evidence

I thought I knew what work was.
I thought I knew what work was
before watching an artist work
at makework in a gallery,
watching a video she made
of herself knocking down a fake
wall in a fake sheet-rocked room
she walled herself in
wearing a red satin dress
and high heels, using a sledge-
hammer to get out, her fake
manual labor making me sweat,
making me mad, making me
self-consciously watch
the museum guard, silent, at his job
watching me watching her
work at her craft. I thought I knew
art work was work at the time,
but just then my dead mother
entered the room
wearing a blue satin dress
she stitched before I was born,
the one she worked
to construct, learning to sew
to please my father.
He sent her to school to learn
how to mend, to keep house, to cook,
her own mother too poor
and beleaguered to teach
much of anything
but honesty. An honest day's work.
And she stood there watching

the guard watching me
watching this artist make art,
all of us working at watching
her knock down a wall
she made for herself.
The only other sound in the room
was my blood knocking arteries
banging their cavities. That was all.
And an occasional cough
from the guard.

Resident

I take steel blue
& titanium white

back to my room.
The prospect of paint

is the refuge
of ideas. The sun loads

the mountain
chestnut

leaves with light,
the other nut

trees stand
in the dark.

Cloudage.
The death of spring

is exposure,
bars of what drops

from the sky,
bands where

the hail falls, then rain,
then night.

"Passione"

I pull your fingers through my hair
at the movies as if we were
both blind, your hand under
mine. Outside, on the street, lovers,
both deaf/mute, were really
going at it. I mean they were
screaming the air
with their hands, their torsos,
their hair. One of their manes
snakes around her as if
in the heat of a seizure. Medusa.
The film is Italian. *Neapolitan*
lava in lyrics, subtitles that leave us
spelling out: *love is a wound that*
continues to grow, it will never
let you go. I know this, I *know*,
loosening my grip, letting your
hand drop to your lap gently
in the dark. On film, Caruso, oh!
oh! All the unbeautiful women
of Naples, broken-hearted, breaking
the hearts they stomp on. That's
Italian, that's what we're told.
A woman smokes, squatting
on a fire escape, flicking a bit of red ash
over our heads. No longer hot.
I know what a volcano is. I know what it is.

Take Another Little Piece

Here, she said, over the cluttered
dinner table. Everyone was busy
drizzling lemon over the grilled carcass
of the fish one of them caught
that afternoon in the swift water
under a slowly rotting bridge
the color of lichen and dried
blood. Her slender fingers
held the coarsest tuber,
a sweet potato or yam.
I can never get it right. *Darling*,
she said to someone else,
though she was looking
at me. The mother of all ferries
slid by the screened-in porch,
dragging with it the view every twelve
minutes. But who's counting?

Pastoral

Sleeping, my body's a Mack truck,
my chassis so heavy it's sunk
into the manured hillside, the grass
knitted to my face. Without shame
my frame penetrates the next level
which is clay, then gravel, then the water
table, the y table, and x, and z

down here where Dante imagined hell to be
I lie, undignified with freight,
saturated in a way that would be art if art
could be made of such sordid un-
enlightenment. Out of earth
so disturbed: wake up, I love you.

Key West: In Relief

Beauty is a plank in the middle
of the ocean the scholar

quotes Augustine and I quote her
from my notes scratched

on paper, the page itself
a ferry, a craft. Who said

when you see something beautiful
you must change your life?

I copy this in an act of
reciprocal aliveness, to be

replicated, later,
without the slideshow, micro-

phone, listeners,
without my friend

nudging me in common
appreciation. What a relief

to see a thing
reflected. Tonight

a sea flea stowed in a shell
in my satchel springs out,

crossing the table,
leaping.

Refuge

Labastide-Esparbairenque

We discover an unfortified village
la bastide, in France,
built by serfs
as a way to be free,
in Occitan *esparbairenque*
is to live outside
the walls of protection.
Our prospects are our
best weapons. We make love
with our faces, our words,
our intentions.

Art/Work

after Kabir

How do you,
asks the guard,
protect a *Landscape*
where there are no trees
or soil;
where satellites
stationed like stars
watch stones and the sea
reproduce freely;
where rain
is transparent
but solid;
where sounds
replace color,
and nothing agrees to
stay on the walls;
where objects
go after ideas?

Does anyone know
what I'm talking about?

About You

There are so many of you:
the lover you, the "ex" lover
you—you, the best friend, you,
the neighbor, the analyst,
driver, co-worker,

the hover-mother you,
the alarm-ringing,
trouble-making,
finger-wagging, never-listening-
to-a-word-I-say *you*. All the you(s)

who are stand-ins for the many me(s),
as referred to in the Second Person
or Third Person, the you I'll call
the "she" I can't stand, I can't live with,
or without, the group "you,"

the sick, and early departed,
the dying and
paralyzingly *alive* you, the one who
disappears when needed,
the you that goes by another name

as in when "you" are a dog,
or a tree, or the sea,
or an implement disguised as a plane
landing, or a pen, or the ink
that leaves clues when it dries;

the Rorschach you: blotted, sobbing,
exposing the all-or-nothing you,
the self-conscious, unconscious
trace of you, the you
when the two of you met, fell in love,

settled for *less* than expected,
got *more* than you bargained for,
the you who cannot spend another day,
another minute, another lifetime
of this *bliss* together,

the you I expected, regretted,
ponderous, careless,
the never-look-back you,
the curious, perseverating,
deal-making, deal-breaking

Pollyanna, sky-is-falling you,
the you who is siren and barker, both
sweet and silent, sometimes
humming a tune no one will ever hear,
or *want* to,

the you so few would *ever* understand
because *that* you, the *real* you,
the original, authentic you
who can only be read in translation,
who is *always* an approximation,

cross-cultural, cross-gendered, *ambi-*
everything, all purpose, visible,
irreplaceable,
admired, abandoned-only-to-be
recovered,

the you who appears
in every poem I ever wrote
or ever will write, the one I love,
am devoted to, the you who needs no
introduction — that's you — just you.

oh well

A streak of white
fell like wet paint
and landed on the back
of her head,
her shoulder,
and slid down her back —
something like a gull
exhaled and left
before landing
on a piling
where a man in a
two-piece yellow slicker
hosed down a rig
infused with
the stink of dead
or dying porgy
carcasses
crated and lining
the Sound side
of the docks.

Even now
I think of her
two years dead,
paint brush in hand
at the beach
or in bed
with nothing on,
the cross on her
forehead
so deep
no one can touch it.

I miss her
and whisper
it doesn't matter
when I try to
keep her alive
and *oh well*,
when I decide not to.
She looks around
for something
to wipe
the gluey white ash
from the nape
of her neck.
Shit – a halo of excrement.

Subjects Matter

Lucien Freud (1922–2011)

For me, the paint is the person.

All morning erasures. First,
my father, then mother.

Now, you. Of the past I grasp
one handful, then the next,

turning my face to the side,
my lips, gills, opening and

closing. I am crawling to a raft
that can only be reached

in my sleep. My hands, eyes,
touch your face, arms drawing

your body in strokes, not just
nude but obtrusively naked.

Suspect

We are always warring over what we can't
touch to see. There's the moon again. Even
absent the moon powers over us the way
dreams do. What would be different if
thoughts were speech? I paint you on the
mowing, knowing you doze each night on a
camp cot looking up. Here the dogged poppy
heads wait to be cut back, leggy, wooden,
dead. Even in this heat the moon drops a
kind of frost, making every thing look the
way love looks losing light, the dark as sharp
as what's lit – with no one to watch over it.

Short Back & Sides

The reason it doesn't hurt
when it's cut is

it's dead, the biologist said,
brushing her dead bangs,

the color of bark,
back from her dead

eyebrows reaching up,
surprised we didn't

know this already. The sushi
came just then,

the wait staff with hair
cut severely,

uniformly straight. The rain
pounced the pavement

aggressively, plashing
back, knocking the plate glass

where we sat sipping sake.
For the first time in months

a smile stretched my lips
till they hurt

and I reached for your
dead gray locks,

curling with impunity
in the humidity

exposing the buds of your
ears. So queer,

the Super Cuts mentality
under discussion.

$20.00. Butch
or femme. *Why spend more*

on something that's dead
you said. *Hair:*

the sexual organ
that shows, someone

read. No wonder we pay.
We love our stylists,

clinging, dependent.
My best friend,

someone said.
How we cried

over a bad color
or cut, evocative locks

severed from their nests.
Our scalps let them go.

Dead anyway, right?
Why should we care?

The temperature rose.
Dead strands,

bleached, and gelled,
blown into place,

hugged one Upper
East Side head

turner, then the next,
gingerly passing by.

Someone shook
an umbrella,

someone shook her head.

Stick

Tonight everyone said yes to a dirty martini before dinner and this didn't seem to prolong or distort the conversation we were having about corn. It turns out every single hairy bit, what we shuck, absentmindedly, on the porch, in the yard, at the sink in the tiny galley kitchen, is attached to a kernel from the start. Each strand we watch, shifting in a breeze, on camera, in life, by the side of the road, is anchored to a pip. On the couch, I sit stroking the silky, slender strands of a memory, a heat wave, shucking corn on a rock, or by a house somewhere else, so hot we peeled off our shirts, and stayed, half dressed, shucking, talking, the moon a trail in the dark. Your old deaf dog, our sole witness, nosed in the leaves licking the filaments with great anticipation and disappointment. So, too, our own. But sometimes between sips, between fields, something. Something.

Knowing

Oh, to travel, to step down
into the sunken lane, to be sunk,
to sink and relish the green
gliss of it. I think of Lucy, who
never passed a lake or a pond,
a sea or a sound
she didn't think to slip into.

After my last dip of the day,
my second swim,
the sun dried the sea to salt
on my skin and I think of her
and imagine I know why she longs to,
at every chance, at every coast – swim.
How the water receives her
unflinching, without judgment.
How her body floats
the way she must have floated in utero –

spineless and mindless at first,
no more than a speck,
the way we'd live if we could
let the phones ring, let the texts go,
be so out of touch,
the small print we can barely read
is barely news at all, a shadow,
a stand in for all that's unsaid,
all that's unfinished, unwritten, unread –
for all that becomes a meadow, a sea, a sound
all fluid, all containment, where the sink,
the pleasure, the knowing and
not knowing, the you in all things comes in.

Poetry & Smoke: A Manifesto

I am for a poetry that makes nothing happen.

I'm for a poetry that's too young to date, but too old to overlook.

I'm for a poetry that wants to paint.

I was thinking of those huge paintings by Francis Bacon at the Metropolitan Museum last summer. There must have been about fifty of them. I was thinking of the colors, the wide open space in them, the intensity of their shapes after the stun gun of subject matter. I was looking at myself looking at the canvases, standing in front of them. I was seeing myself, later, in his studio, in the chaos of it. I was thinking of his workspace in relation to his work. Order from disorder. I'm for a poetry that *makes order from disorder*. And sometimes *takes it back*.

There's pleasure in some kinds of confinement, like, say, a correctional facility *of your own design*. But that's not what a poem is in my book, not exactly, not a correctional facility. I believe poems come from confinement, quarters you make and inhabit for a while. You have to find a good place to spin like the silk worms in the stalls on the dusty side streets of Shanghai. They spin themselves into an elegant net for display, for the tourists. And the net is all a person can see standing there on the sidewalk, not the worms, which aren't really worms at all, but invisible markers that turn into moths, or become a shell of themselves in a jar on a shelf.

I'm for a poetry that sets out to make something clear, something *visually, sonically, spatially pleasing*. Not opaque. Not obscure. Not overly sensual, either. Not cloying the way X's poems are (do I have to name names?) overly rhymed, inside and out, sensual for sensuality's sake, poems that fall all over themselves, that make out with themselves, loving themselves and the sounds they make way too much, so there's no room, no love left for the reader. I'm for the reader. I'm for leaving some room for the reader, a lot of room.

I'm for a poetry that is tart, that barks a little, and maybe, sometimes, *a lot*, a poetry that calls attention to itself ... but ... then leaves you alone. You know, the way you feel when the neighbor's dog down the hall has finally stopped barking. And there's suddenly silence. And you never thought of silence that way before, of the word: *silence*. But there you are on the couch, grateful to the damn dog for barking, the dog you were, moments before, dreaming of feeding a bad ham to. But now you *love* that dog, because now you can practically *taste silence* in the wake of his bark, a new taste, one you never tasted before.

And speaking of taste, I'm also for a poetry that still smokes. A poetry that sends signals, words that are signs with their smells still attached, a little ash, a little resin, still sticky, still holding onto their scorched antecedents. I'm for words arranged in a way that makes you think about where they come from, word origins, words that take you back to the beginning of something, even if it isn't their *real* beginnings, the places they *actually* come from, but an original place, one you imagined into being. I'm for words that were orphans until you gave them a sentence.

DRIVE

[the most beautiful thing]

The most beautiful thing about my car is the beach, and the most beautiful thing about the beach is watercolor, and the most beautiful thing about water is the word, and the most beautiful thing about the word is pigment, and the most beautiful thing about pigment is the soil, and the most beautiful thing about soil is the earth, and the most beautiful thing about the earth is the sea, and the most beautiful thing about the sea is the drive.

This

for H.S.

In the way your poem
with a lake in it
is not about the lake, mine
with a dog and the broken
heart is not about a dog
or saving face. Your ibis as pearls
in their nests is no more
about the sway of banyan trees
than it is about lovers and brothers
or fathers living among
the cedars
and scat in my poems, nor
those pyres by the tracks
waiting for a match, all
queerly remembered, queer
as teaching ourselves
not to drown, or of clouds
that don't move, what a sea hawk
carries in her talons,
and the long dirt road,
and the navel of the moon?
All poems about storms at sea,
combined, are not about
the earth's proclivities, but
deciding what spins.
Everything is about
gravity, the grave
pulling
for us. Each day
it starts with a bark
calling our name.

Drive

My tiny car's tiny engine
groans and hums
the way my mother hummed

a little ditty when
nervous,
the way I do

mulling over something hard
letting my chest
send a message

to my mouth, my mouth
forming a kind of growl
while all along

staying shut. I enter
the on-ramp to the freeway
heading home

from a family visit,
the pedal to the floor,
I pump my chin

toward the dashboard
thinking I'm helping.
I think I hear

my brother's taunt:
What is it
with women

and cars? We are old,
old enough,
to equate mobility

with independence.
Real wheels
take me out of state,

escaping the trap
I thought was
the small town. For this

I left the ocean
I left the trees
I left Eel Pond with seabirds

standing on spring ice,
summer surfboards lined up
on the berm

between the sea grass
and the sea.
I left my family of origin,

my Lucky buried in the back-
yard, dog heaven,
now home to a chalet

built by strangers,
the chicken coop,
the barn, gone. When

driving I think of love
as a road trip, the soaring,
the breakdown, jump-

starts, the brand new,
and old reliable.
I'm no mechanic

though I once knew
how to change a fan belt
sheared to a thread.

Here the air is fresh.
The new mutt
who travels with me

leaves her nose prints
on the passenger windows
the way my old dog did,

leaving a spot
just clear enough
to drive through.

Self-Portrait: Between the Car and the Sea

I think I'll stay blonde
a while longer. Downshifting
for the view, today,

the engine strains
in first gear the way
on foot my body

climbing the last few steps
does. You'd hear it, too,
if the heart

had a literal voice. Silently
pulling for itself,
the will wants the body to

give it what it wants.
How long will these parts last?
I put off minding the flags

lifting their faces. I watch sea lice flit
from shell to sand to beach
eased by transition lenses.

Fuel

My stealth self
wants to know
what I am driving at

when I say *drive*. I idle,
touching the ignition
now that a car

needs no key,
no handler,
not even

me. I reach for the stick
shift, the hand-
break, the choke,

retrieve an imaginary
clutch. No passenger
knows

what a driver knows,
her grip
on the wheel, foot

on the pedal,
flat
to the floor. My hand

to eye equals
foot to gut
coordination. Speed

equals oxygen
to the brain. The dead
ends of my hair

dragged through the air,
pull their roots
alive. Did she say

or did I say
drive?

Ignition

I remember my hand
on the car's smooth blue

lining, the Rambler's
door as it opened

to the damp grass
of the lawn

to the new house.
I was three

close to four
years old, my father,

newly dead
and my mother

just learning
to drive.

How to Draw a Heart

The arteries of the turbine as seen from the train are actively compressing *god knows what* as we shuttle past Deer Park Station. I think I read it was jet fuel to fuel engines, and jet engine components produced here, parts as small as the smallest rotors for dental drills to full scale motor armatures like those of the heart, which is as close to a turbine as anything else in the body. I guess the stomach, too, is a turbine but I don't see the stomach illustrated on any Hallmark cards, no doily-accompanied tubes to say *I love you* though the stomach is really the first to know if something's up before the heart kicks in, the engines to the intimate holding infinitely complex hinges that swing with desire. We keep trying to illustrate desire as if desire were something one could draw as an expression of love, something possible to construct.

Nonplace

That spring before I met you
I found myself
in a tiny white rental car
with a moon-roof
and stick shift
in a country where
I didn't speak
the language
on a roadway
whose names and numbers
didn't match
my Baedeker
nor the *quaint* idea
to bring a map
that belonged to my father
who died
young.

And I could swear
he joined me
skirting foothills
we explored
decades earlier
on a family trip
in an American Oldsmobile
abroad
though I have no way
to prove we drove
this same route.

Maybe the past is not
the way to navigate. So strong
the impulse
to make place
personal. But this was it
my non-
place
the off hours
days alone

my body blessed
with little significance
without lover without friends
no family
nor possibility
of conversation
so little familiar

even the gas pump presented
a craving for intelligence
a marker
coming and going
craving and
caving
heaven on earth
coming
and for god's sake
going.

Copper Beech

Because it had been, quite literally,
four decades since I last climbed a tree
I stood a long while watching you
overhead. Your elbows disappeared
in the sheets of plum-dark leaves,
so cool in the heat. I pressed
my face against the bark, I patted
your dog's snout – lost – my body touching
the idea of leaving earth. I wrapped
my arms around a trunk wider than
my own, growth and decay in my mouth.
I kissed the twins, fear and ecstasy,
my feet where my shoulders
once were. My fingers reached
for the sole of your shoe. A blanket of green
held me in its arms, the backsides
of leaves last seen from the ground.

A Thing or Two

The leaf falls on the page,
red after being green

her whole life. The mail carrier
and his broken marriage

at the door deliver grief
and the *Paris Review*,

the icemaker knocking out
ice. Outside the trees laugh

the tops of their heads off.
This blow, a breeze, gusts

wildly denuding
deciduous trees, determined

to leave nothing weak behind.
Oblivious, the pines

have grown too close
to the shingled house.

They brush the slats.
Both are cedar and flirt

with reunification. We live
by the sea and clear-cut trees

harvested for building
and burning. Some die

for others, and by some
I mean those who don't breathe

the way we do, but are no less
alive: beach grass, trees, the breeze.

Dear trees — the earth still spins
for the love of you. I lean my skin

against your skin. My dog
in all innocence pees

at your feet. I let him.
Your mourning arouses — *x* —

in the air, what I breathe
and can't breathe,

what I see and don't — but want to.

[ride]

The most beautiful thing about a convertible is hair, and the most beautiful thing about hair is its disposition, dead, but alive in the skin in the air, the skin holding on to each strand for dear life, alive in the wind. The most beautiful thing about the wind passing over the skin is sensation, cellular, invisible, metabolic. What is metabolic is life-sustaining, and the most life-sustaining thing I can think of today is decency. And decency is blind, unseen, until it isn't.

Transport

I don't expect the end
to be like the din of a river,
a sound
with no beginning.

I'm certain the end is the sea.
Not the sound of the sea,
but the sea itself,
the part that expires

after it heaves. You
may think the sea draws a breath
and comes back, but
the *what* of it ends

in a wave. There is an end
to a wave. That's my view,
my range, those are my thoughts
as they downshift from sky

to road to sea in a Fiat
which struggles to power
its way into Spain
over the steep pitch

of the coast road, the nervous
gear-shift clicking in such a way
I begin to wonder
where I left my Last Will

& Testament. Cresting each peak,
I conjure the names
of my family, of friends on signage
before the road drops

into the perfect dark O
blasted into a neck
of a cliff, reeling
from black out back into the light,

into the vineyards, perpendicular
to the one-lane highway,
the grape leaves so close
they graze the car's door

skirting sharp curves,
as I become the sea
become the horizon.
Driving alone –

voices in my head –
wait to be heard,
those dying to speak,
enter the car

the windows wide open:
I can't believe
you chose this road
one says. Another's

matches the twiggy vines
knotted
in the dry brown earth
like ties to a quilt. One

counts syllables,
sensory signals on signposts
in three languages
whizzing by. Another

searches the rear-view
mirror, thinking out loud:
watch that biker
cycling too close to the car.

When the GPS enters
the conversation,
my voices
jam behind a jack-knifed truck—

KAFKA TRANSPORT S.A.—
in block letters on its cab—
a voice suggests we turn back
five kilometers.

I see what the GPS
cannot. She,
with the British accent
and satellite vectors:

this detour is really a path.
Can I still fix a flat? I ask
the empty car
trying to remember

the last vehicle ... the last person
passed after leaving
the paved roads. Alone (together)
we climb a ridge

that had been blocking the view
all along, behind which
are white-capped hilltops
a vast valley, unpassable

below. The window open,
I feel for the air, sweet and slow.
Daylight pours over my face,
my lap. I thank then curse

no one, backing up
a few thousand yards,
skidding and dipping
spilling the useless

map, notes, water
from a cup. I imagine
my hair at a slant, cartoon-
style, watching my wallet

slide out of sight. *Alone
and in a circumstance*
without losing my way
my shirt might

still be dry, but I might never
have considered a soft
fall from a cliff,
among poppies

so red they recompose red
in vines so faint they are
practically white,
so tangled they conjugate

the verb *to tangle*
a new way, the way
green tangles into
the crease of the rocks,

the way the Mediterranean
tangles into cloud cover
turning a shade
that could never be made

by hand. I see
how the road ruts now,
the way it twists
as I backed

all the way down
to a seedy town, taking
time, something I can
handle and untangle, here,

now, without a watch.

Landscape with Power Lines

The twisting cords, no longer
bother me. As I see it,
they heighten the light, halved

and halved again, leaves and clouds, snow
and storm. The breeze moves an olive branch
over one line, then another below. Each branch

acts as if her leaves aren't about to be swayed
to stay on one side for good. They remain
undecided. Today they are subject to a dust

kicked up as a truck hauling crops powers past.
Birds make their wild plans to nest
one last time. They weave their sticks

and tissue their housing
including these lines.
We are bound to live together.

My Dead

brother returns as
the old man in the sea
surfing. The waves change,

but always change
in the same way. My brother
will always be a comma

in a sea of commas,
a pause in the loose
language of waves

seen from shore. He will always be
too far away to read, as close
as the salt on my skin

is — like his skin — that dries
and flakes.
And shadows him.

Sew

The surgeon still binds
our wounds the way
cave dwellers

cinched woolly capes
and caps, viscous
and weave –

the original thread,
the first needle, pig's gut,
heron's beak chiseled

to the size of a wick
with an eye. I wonder
how my mother

seamed her desires –
her sewing, her rudder,
the hum and glow,

pedal below,
how she learned to drive,
a widow alone

in a small-town wilderness,
object-oriented. Her making
my own.

Self as Hypotaxis

By which I mean, ego is hierarchical,
X is better than Y. Today
is better than this same day in May

last year. I am happier than I was
when spring equaled death,
so many wakes, so many silences,

equal and un-equal. Spring
sometimes operates
in opposition

to her contract with the earth, and
is not always the birth
of something good. The earth asserts

all seasons be different
but equal. Each a beauty. Maybe
the earth has a preference. Summer,

after all, is generally queen.
I doubt I am alone
in singling out late June

by the sea,
as heaven on earth.
The earth warms,

and not in a threatening way.
The worms brave
the earth's skin's surface

moving through turf
after a rain, free. And even if
it hasn't rained since spring

the flags of my disposition
are happiest in summer, that is to say,
greener, and fresher. And softer longer.

Autobiographia Literaria

after Frank O'Hara

Someday the blank page will rush
under me and with the grace

of a walk in the woods
with you, who have been silent

for years. You will blow sun
in the spring-leafed trees,

and the damp earth
will begin to dry

and crack, and the birds
who no longer migrate

will start to sing, despite
global warming, for they, too

love the author, who stumbles
through time. Still, there's a chance

that history repeating itself
will change course. *You're not*

dead yet, a friend who has
passed liked to say, and

I've been known
to perseverate. And repeat, and repeat,

and will probably do so
from the grave, my stone

etched with the text: Not yet.
Not yet.

[trust]

The scraps of text on papyrus, dry as dirt, attributed to Sappho, are pinned in place by the tiniest strips of archival tape. I had never seen adhesive so delicate, so *trusted*. The most beautiful thing about trust is what holds it in place.

ACKNOWLEDGMENTS

I am deeply grateful to the editors and publishers and staff of the following journals, websites, blogs, anthologies, and textbooks where some these poems first appeared, at times in different versions.

NEW POEMS
Cutleaf: "Time," "Screen Door"; *Five Points*: "Incandescence," "Memory Theatre"; *On the Seawall*: "When It's Good to Stop Talking"; *Ploughshares*: "Poetry"; *The Red Wheelbarrow*: "Tension"; *Upstreet*: "Flight"; *Wildwood*: "Site Specific," "The Work of Art"; SWWIM: "Small Points"; *Touchstone (Poetry Society of New Hampshire)*: "3 a.m."; *The Westchester Review*: "Grey Scales," "Last Night in the Country."

FROM SLEUTH
American Poetry Review, The Christian Science Monitor, Connect, 5 a.m., Frigate, Hubbub, The Marlboro Review, Mars Hill Review, New Letters, On the Page, Prairie Schooner, Rattapallax, Rivendell, River Styx, The Women's Review of Books, You Are Here: The Journal of Creative Geography. Anthologies: IOU: *New Writing on Money* (Concord Free Press), *Raising Lilly Ledbetter: Women Poets Occupy the Workplace* (Lost Horse Press), *Wake Up Grateful* (Storey Publishing).

FROM CAUSEWAY
American Poetry Review, Barrow Street, Bellevue Literary Review, Bloom, Global City Review, Hawaii Pacific Review, Hubbub, Mantis: A Journal of Poetry, Criticism, and Thought, O! The Oprah Magazine, Poetry, Poetry Daily, The Massachusetts Review, New Letters, River Styx, Upstreet, The Women's Review of Books. Anthologies & Sites: *Rabbit Ears: Poems About T.V.*, (NYQ Press), *From the Fishouse* (Fishouse Poems).

FROM PROSPECT/REFUGE
About Place Journal, Barrow Street, Big City Lit, Bloom, Connotation Press, The Cossack Review, Fogged Clarity, Hamilton Stone Review, Hunger Mountain, Indolent Books, Ocean State Review, Plume, Promethean, Sinister Wisdom, Two Rivers Review, Salamander, Upstreet. Anthologies and Textbooks: *The Practice of Creative Writing* (Bedford/St. Martins), *Rabbit Ears* (NYQ Press), *Nasty Women Poets* (Lost Horse Press), *World English Poetry* (Bengal Foundation).

FROM DRIVE
AMP *(Hofstra University Press), Cordite Poetry Review, Five Points, Global City Review, The Night Heron Barks, Ocean State Review, On the Seawall, Plume, Rattle, Upstreet.* Anthologies: *Treelines: An Anthology of 21st Century American Poems* (Grayson Books), *I Wanna Be Loved By You* (Milk & Honey Press), *Stronger Than Fear: Poems of Empowerment, Compassion, and Social Justice* (Cave Moon Press).

I owe an enormous debt to the late Herbert S. Scott, founding editor of New Issues, who published my first book of poetry, *Sleuth*; to William Olsen, who finished editing of my second book, *Causeway*, and published it with New Issues (Western Michigan University); to the late Stanley Moss, editor of *Prospect/Refuge* (Sheep Meadow Press); and to the excellent Elizabeth Murphy, editor of *Drive* (Grid Books).

I want to thank the culture workers and organizations, residencies, and retreats, whose support resulted in many of the poems in this collection, including Hedgebrook, the Hermitage Artist Retreat, Monson Arts, Ragdale Foundation, Siena Art Institute, Tyrone Guthrie Centre, and La Muse: Artists and Writers Retreat; and a special thanks the many artists and writers, teachers, and friends, living and not, whose work and lives inspired me. I am grateful to the critics, interviewers, bloggers, podcasters, radio hosts, and influencers, many of whom are writers and poets, for taking the time from their own work to create a wider audience for mine.

To the dedicated poets and writers in my peer review writing group, to the life-sustaining community of writers I teach and collaborate with in 2 Horatio; to Courtney Gillette, director of the Sarah Lawrence College Writing Institute, my home as a teacher for two decades. To my editor Elizabeth Murphy, for her thoughtful and brilliant work on this book, and for the standard of excellence she maintains with the press. Gratitude to John Kramer for his keen eye, and exceptional attention to detail and sublime design. Special thanks to Amy Sillman for permission to use *A Shape that Stands Up and Listens, #26*, which appears on the cover of this book.

To my dearest friends and colleagues, too numerous to mention by name, but without whom there would be less love, less angst, less joy, and less *life* in these poems. And finally, to my beloved life partner and spouse, Nora. This book is dedicated to her.

In "The Work of Art," the italicized text is by the art critic Michael Kimmelman, describing a painting by Duncan Hannah (not the painting in the poem).

In "figure & ground," the author of the epigraph is lost to me. My best guess is David Sedaris or Spalding Gray, but no advanced search resulted in making that link.

"Poetry" is for Ron Slate

"Small Points" is for John Kramer and Daniel McCusker

"Tension" is in memory of my brother William Sexton (1956–2022), and for Judy Fuller

"Still Working" is for Jennifer Stewart Miller

"When It's Good to Stop Talking" is for Teddy Laurel

"*Sound + Color*" is for Laura Kaminsky and Rebecca Allan

MARINA KIRIAKOU

ELAINE SEXTON is a maker, critic, teacher, and micro-publisher. *Site Specific: New & Selected* is her fifth collection of poetry. Her poems are widely anthologized and published in journals including *American Poetry Review*, *Poetry*, *Ploughshares*, and *O! the Oprah Magazine*. She has written the libretto for *The Post Office*, a chamber opera in poems, in collaboration with composer Laura Kaminsky, commissioned by Queen City Opera and developed by Opera Fusion: New Works/Cincinnati Opera. She lives in New York and teaches at the Sarah Lawrence College Writing Institute.

COLOPHON

The poems in this collection are set in Fern, a Venetian Oldstyle typeface designed by David Jonathan Ross originally for the screen. Its diagonal stress, however, and its chunky, triangular serifs, give it a rich and contemporary texture ideal for the setting of poetry in ink on paper. It is a variable font with axes for weight and optical size. (2018)

The front cover, part titles, and section heads are set in Hex Franklin, a sans serif by Nick Sherman — his homage to the classic Franklin Gothic type family. Hex Franklin is also a variable font, with axes of weight and width. (2022)

MORE PRAISE FOR ELAINE SEXTON

ABOUT SLEUTH

"When I first saw Elaine Sexton's poems, I was impressed by their bright intelligence, their fierce gaze and crisp language. Now I see she was always the *Sleuth* intent on knowing the mysteries – and it's that hard bright gaze that redeems the ordinary sorrow in this book and celebrates, without sentimentality, the restorative love here too." MARIE HOWE

"'Could I get more specific?' Elaine Sexton asks rhetorically in a poem about her mother selling the *World Book* door-to-door. The charm of this first book is indeed its specificity. Poem after poem unfolds with crisp detail and subtle metaphors that take us by surprise. 'Nothing,' she writes, 'is safe from poetry,' and with a sure hand she proves it."
MAXINE KUMIN

"Sexton allows her imagery to carry the weight of such difficult emotional themes as the death of a parent or the loss of religious conviction. The poet recounts memories with such aching precision in *Sleuth* that readers will undoubtedly savor the resulting feast."
DANIEL PINKERTON, *Valparaiso Poetry Review*

ABOUT CAUSEWAY

"In their plainspoken engagement with the actual world, Elaine Sexton's poems are models of scrupulous attention, alert to the simple truth that everything is 'part of some bigger mystery' so even a fish can sing a 'psalm,' a simple shoe be the subject of one. The poems in this impressive second collection contain the sound of a consciousness meditating on what is passing in the world and abiding in the heart and mind. Elegy without sentimentality seems a natural part of Sexton's keen-eared lyric manner and, in every sense, responsibility." EAMON GRENNAN

"'Happiness in love, what a joke,' Paul Eluard wrote to Gala in a letter dated 6 March, 1933, and three-quarters of a century later Elaine Sexton, in her second superb volume, struggles against such cynicism in poems that address 'every estuary' of love – filial love, romantic love, spiritual love – without refusing 'to taste the grit.' Again and again the poet attempts to reconcile herself to 'the everyday obscene,' always 'searching for home / in a thrift shop find, something a mother, / not yours or mine, left behind.'" MICHAEL WATERS

"There is no shortage of tension in *Causeway*. ... The work offers a set of thematic and material oppositions: city and country/seaside, intimacy and separation, anxiety and composure, the desire to get things right grating on the sense that something's amiss."
RON SLATE, *On the Seawall*

"Tension infused in small moments becomes radiant as Sexton confidently leads us back into the concrete middle ground. The non-epiphany becomes an entity into itself, playful or woeful. I find the poems in *Causeway* to be much like perfect storms; a slice of ordinary life where, with absolutely no warning, in the blink of an eye, all is transformed."

ALISON WOODS, *Big City Lit*

"Sexton [has a] keen ear for her craft. The poems of *Causeway* sound beautiful. The collection overall is inflected by attention to form. ...While the liminal space between land and sea might seem to dominate the collection, the 'naturalness' of those spaces is in tension with the urban, or 'human-made,' landscapes in which the poet often finds herself."

JULIE ENSZER, *Lambda Book Review*

ABOUT PROSPECT/REFUGE

"Her smart manifesto, 'Poetry and Smoke' proclaims, 'I'm for a poetry that makes order from disorder. And sometimes takes it back.' What she takes it back to, aside from the faceted self, is a kind of nakedness where the self is free from the clichés of gender and beauty and a truer more vulnerable human comes forward. *Prospect/Refuge* is an insightful, well-crafted book that puts Elaine Sexton among the best poets writing now."

ROGER MITCHELL

"In her third, most agile collection, Elaine Sexton not only makes 'order from disorder and sometimes takes it back,' but also divulges a private periodic table that makes the reader privy to hidden elements of being—read it and delight!"

JESSICA GREENBAUM

"Elaine Sexton lovingly crafts her poems with an attention to language that is painterly and agile, intimate and tender. She effortlessly records her observations and thoughts with a Zen-like ease. She is the consummate painter of language, whose airy breadth leaves one to hear the simple music of her poems long after they have finished."

WALTER HOLLAND, *Pleiades Book Review*

"There are hints in *Prospect/Refuge* that the price of clarity means losing the cushion of delusion. Those moments wipe the slate of expectation clean with their unexpected imagery and give optimal impact to longing in all its forms."

LYNN MCGEE, *Lambda Literary Review*

About Drive

"In this dazzling collection, Elaine Sexton brings a life lived in poetry to a startling new premise: acceleration equals exhilaration. These poems make me long for the road in America, foot on the pedal and heart in the wind."
Jeet Thayil

"Great poets teach us to see in words, moments, actions, emotions, and Elaine Sexton does this so vividly and visually that the reader, this reader, is there, with her on her *Drive*. Continually inventive, often startling, the poems in this beautiful collection are a gift for writers, artists, and anyone who loves language."
Jonathan Santlofer

"One of the delights of *Drive* is how Sexton puts her poems together like beads on a string, each string having its own theme. She then weaves the individual strings into a winding helix that beautifully evokes the complexities and vantage point derived from decades of living."
Diane Schenker, *Big City Lit*

"For all *Drive*'s engagement with non-place, the ephemeral and moving between states, time, and place, it's a triumph in crafting the moving image, an affirmation that human connection is the most beautiful thing."
SK Grout, *Night Heron Barks*

"Sexton perfectly describes the exhilaration of a foot on the gas with hands on the steering wheel, feeling a sense of autonomy and power."
Benjamin Schmidt, *At the Inkwell*